Fire! F

Story by Beverley Randell
Illustrated by Crissie Davies

2

"Fire! Fire!" shouted all the Browns.

4

5

The Browns got into the helicopter.

Kit got out and ran away.

Up went the helicopter.

It landed, and all the Browns got out.

The helicopter went back to the fire with a big bucket of water.

Down went the water.

The helicopter came back
again and again and again.

The fire went out.

Hello, Mr. Brown.
The fire is out.
Your home is safe.
I'm coming to get you all.

The Browns went home in the helicopter.

Thank you. Thank you.

14

They looked and looked for Kit.

Look down here!
Here she is.
Kit is safe after all.
Good!

16